This Book Belongs To

. . . .

A Millionaire Trader

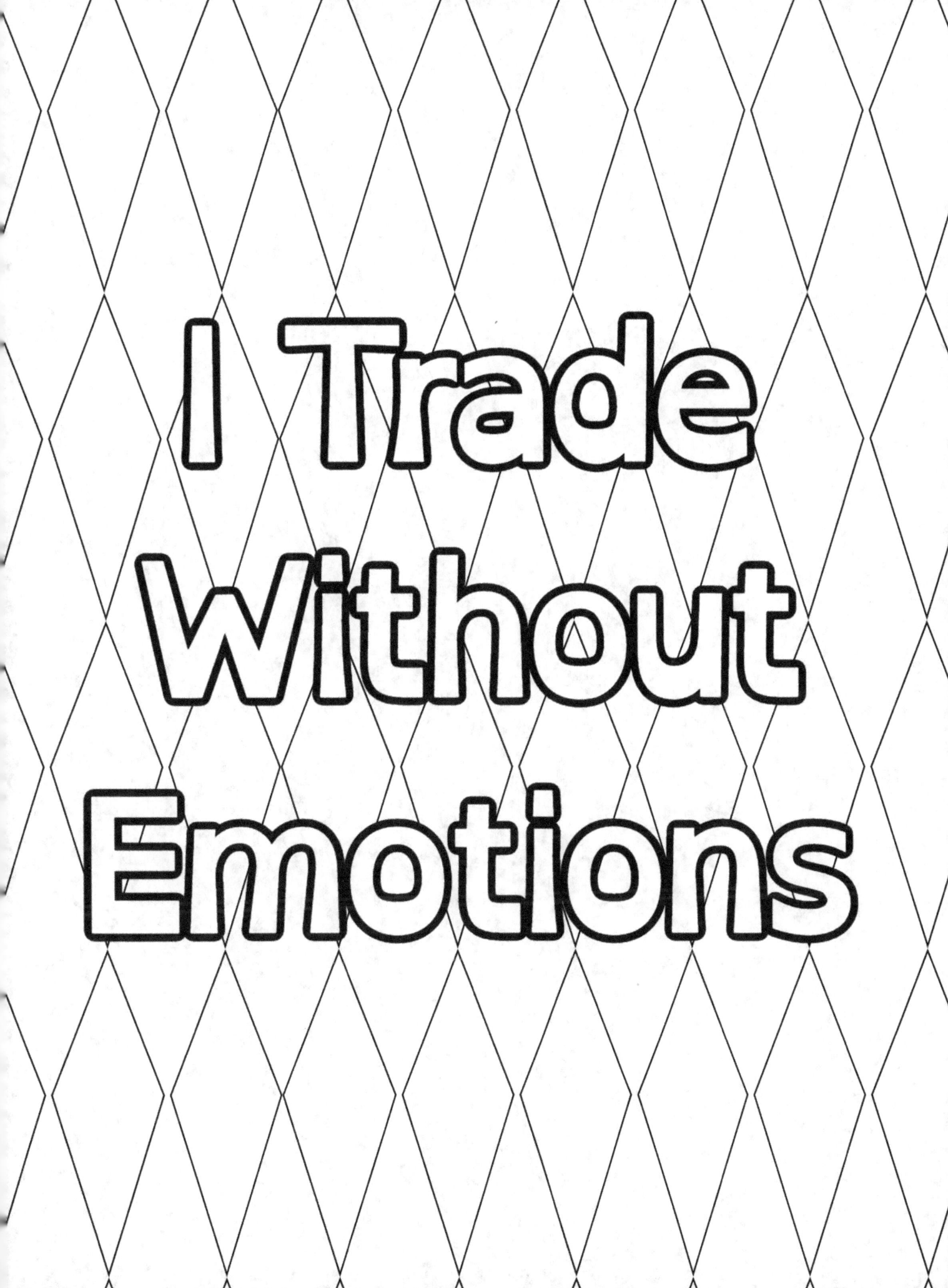

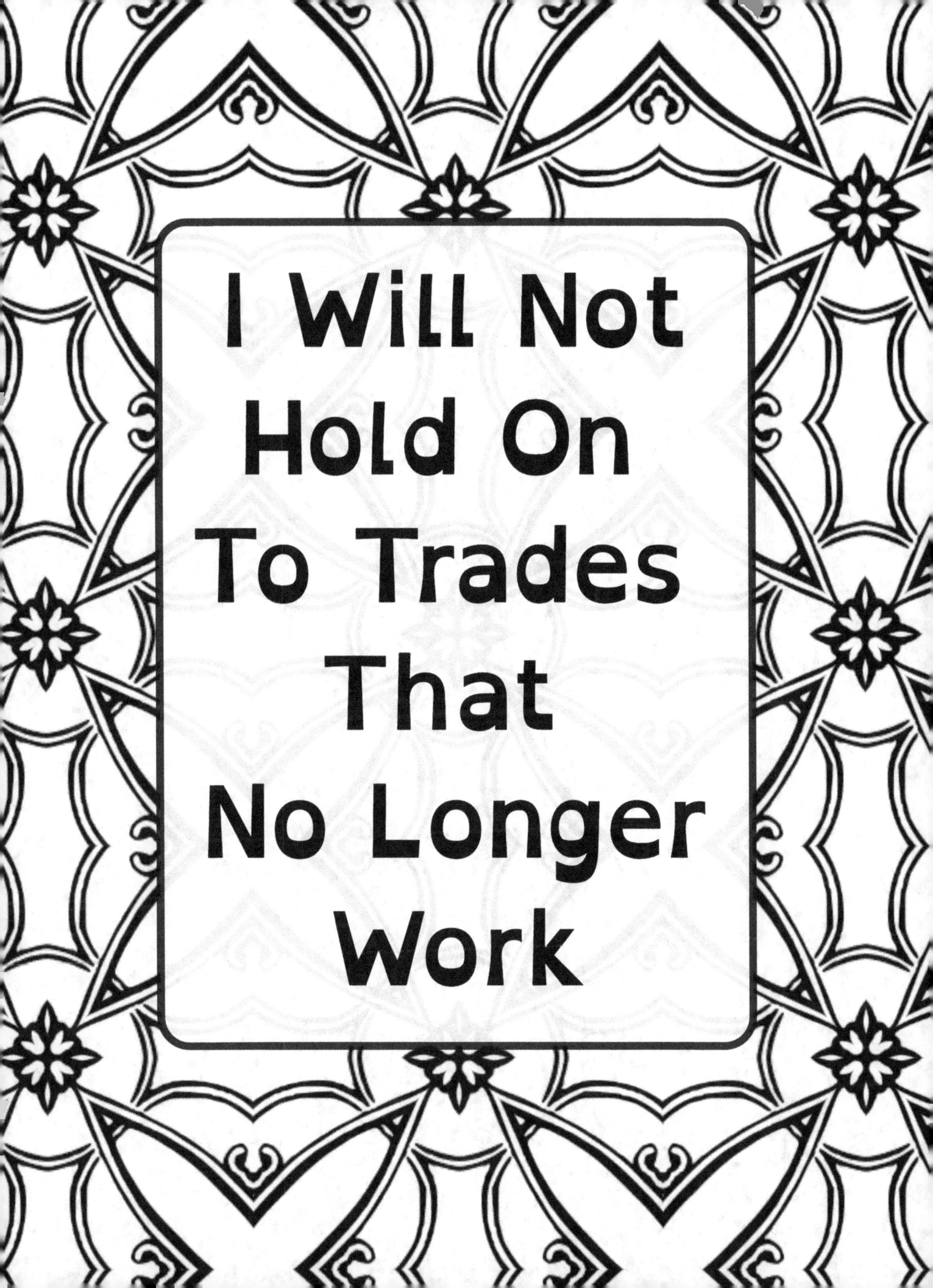

I Will Not Hold On To Trades That No Longer Work

ZOOM OUT & LOOK At The BIG PICTURE

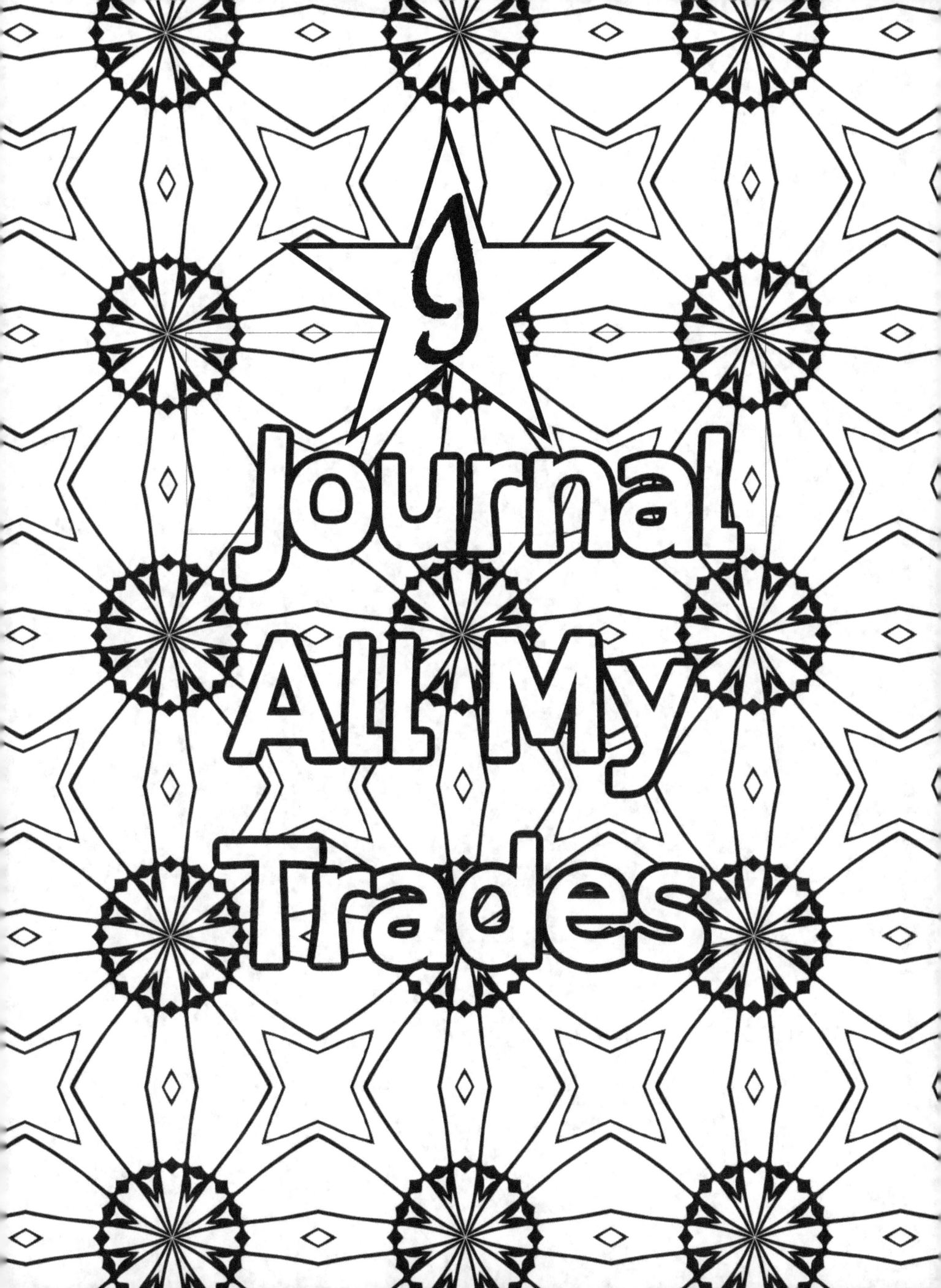

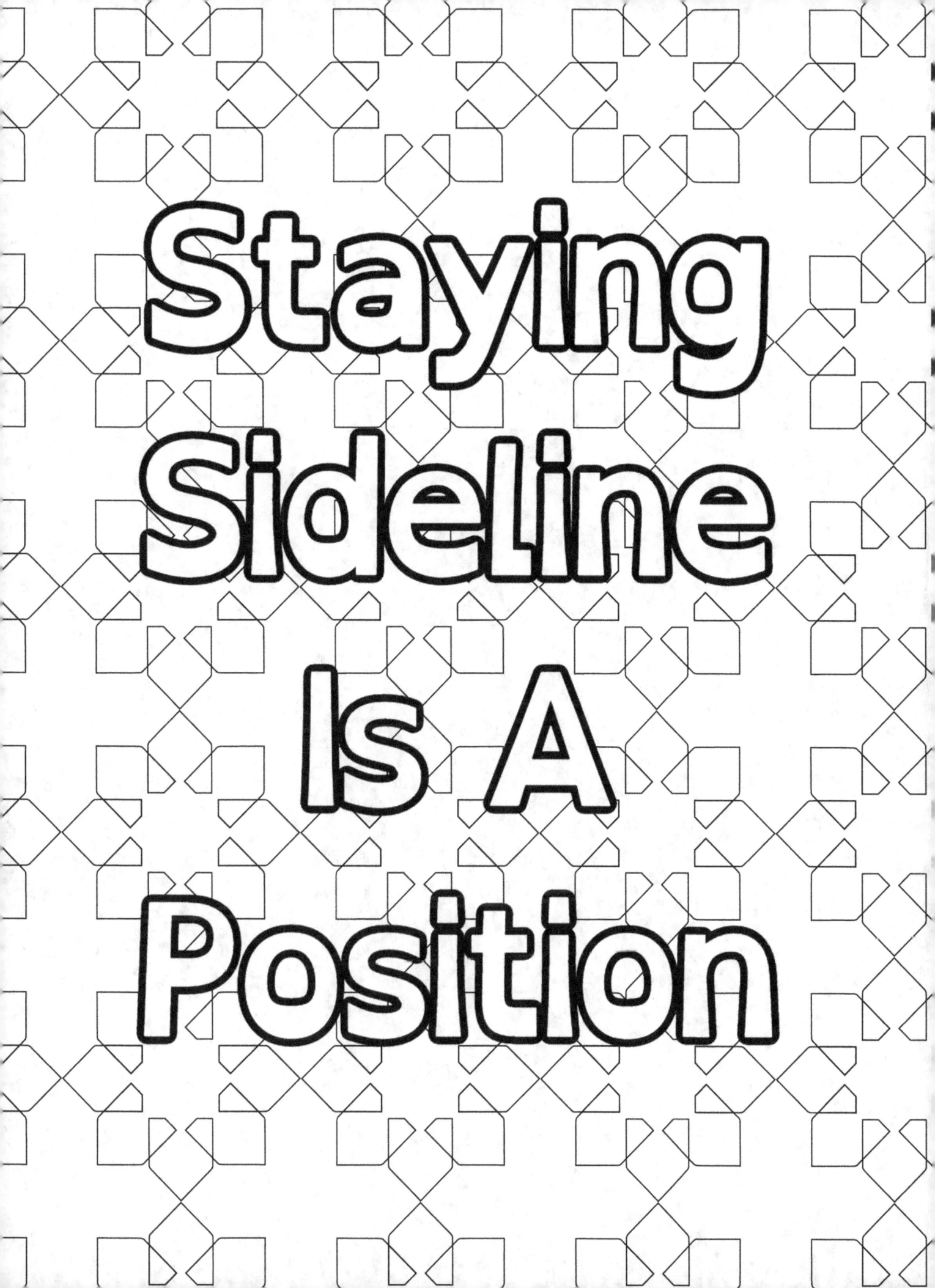

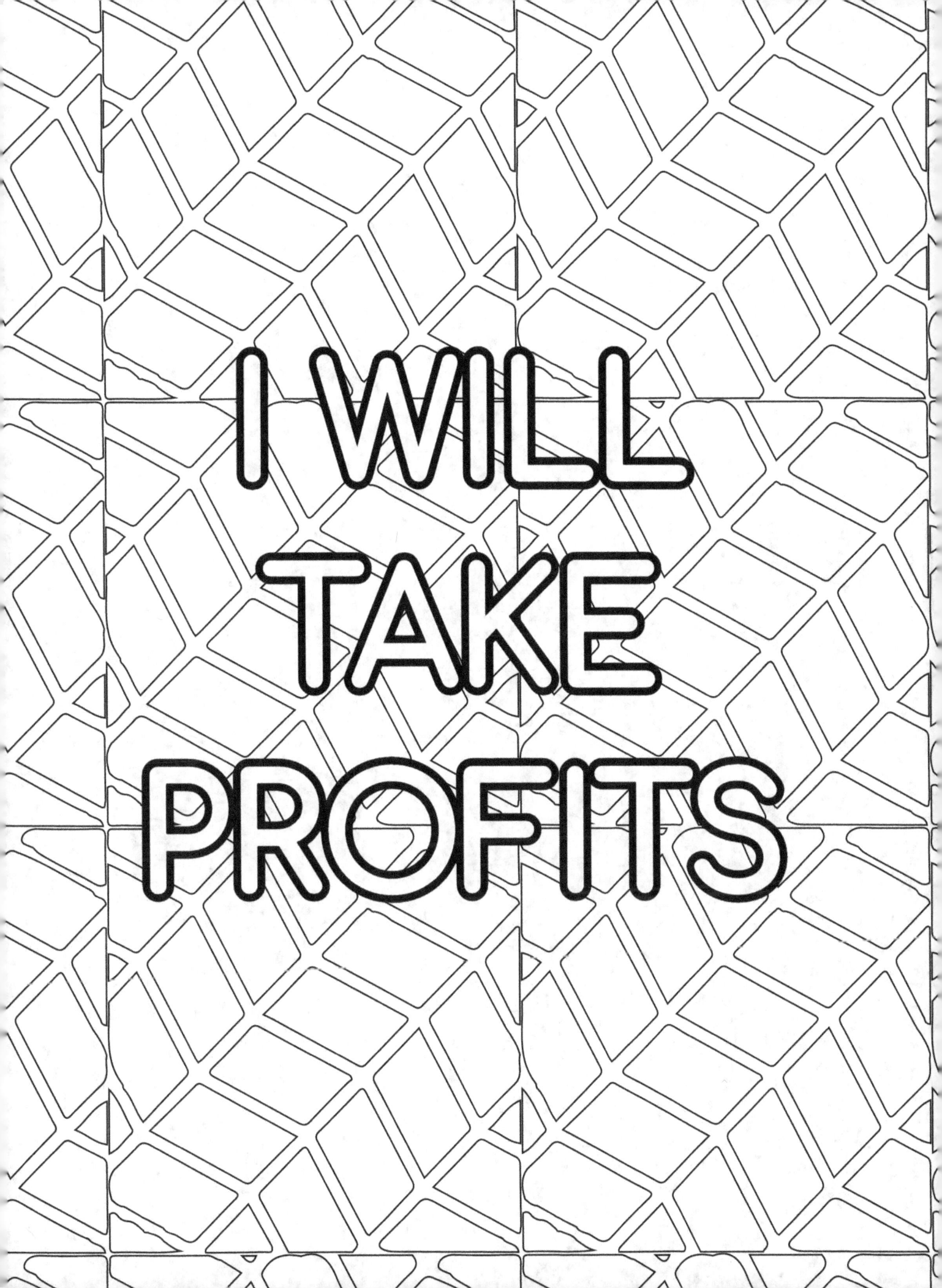

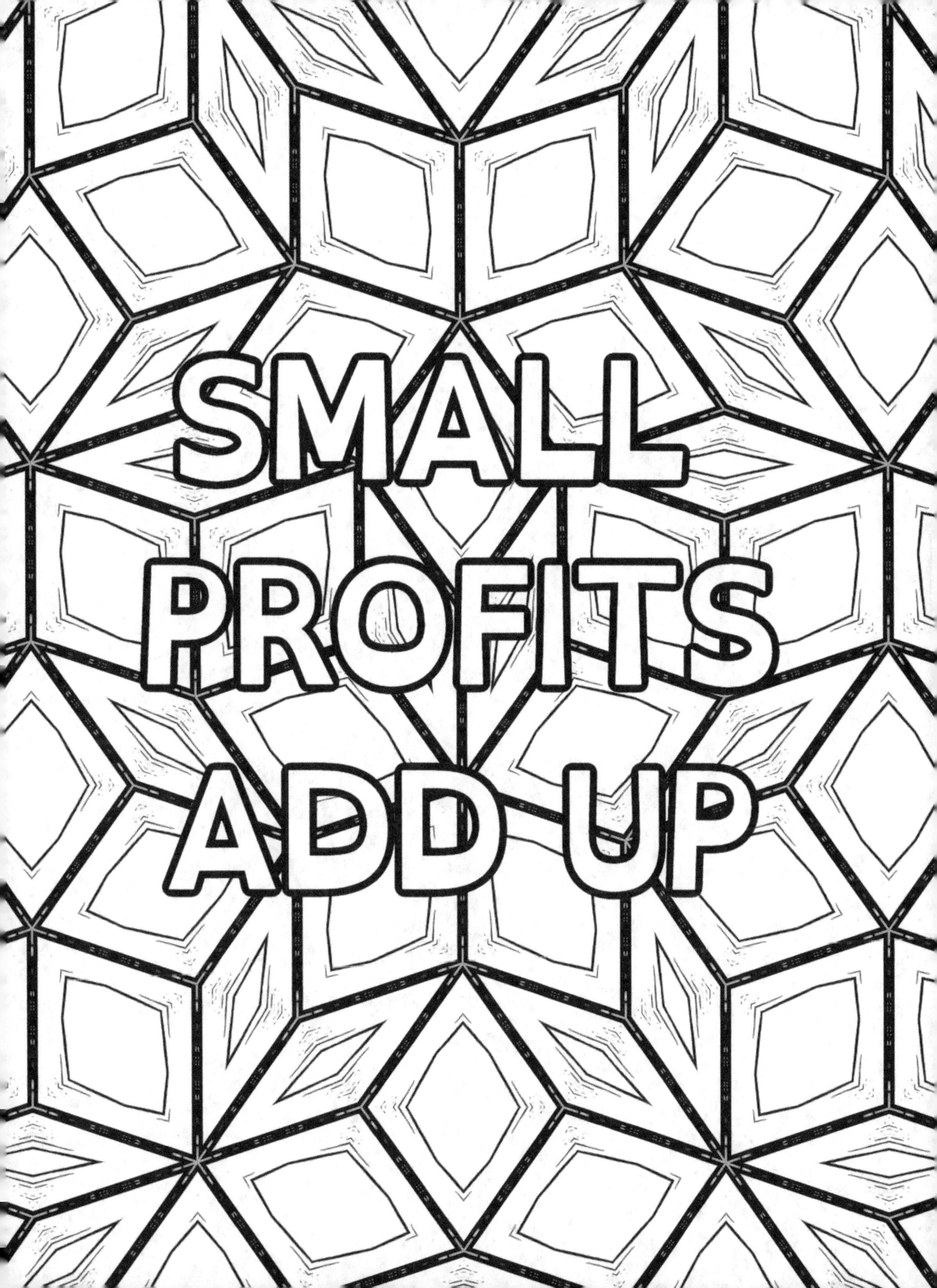

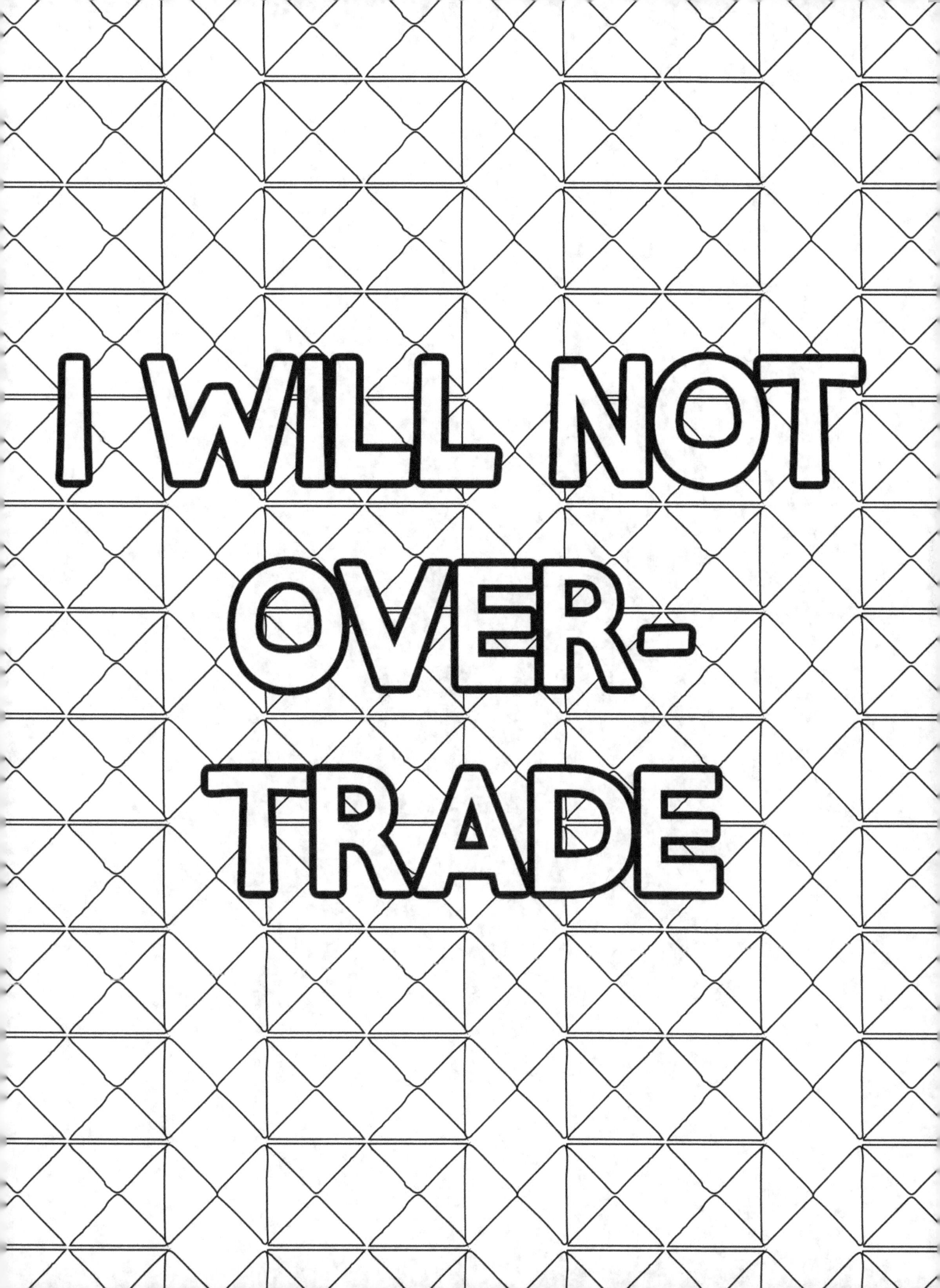

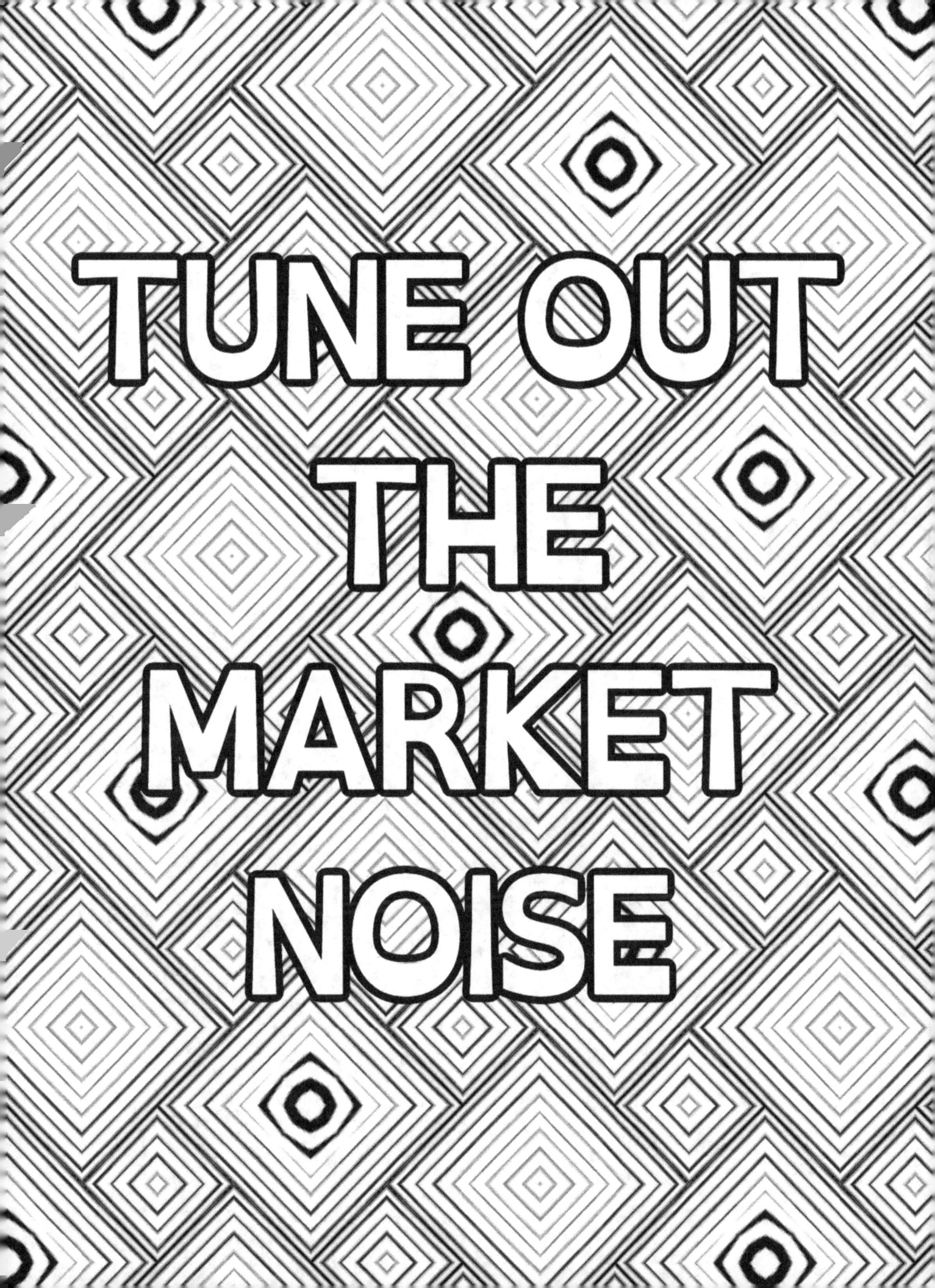

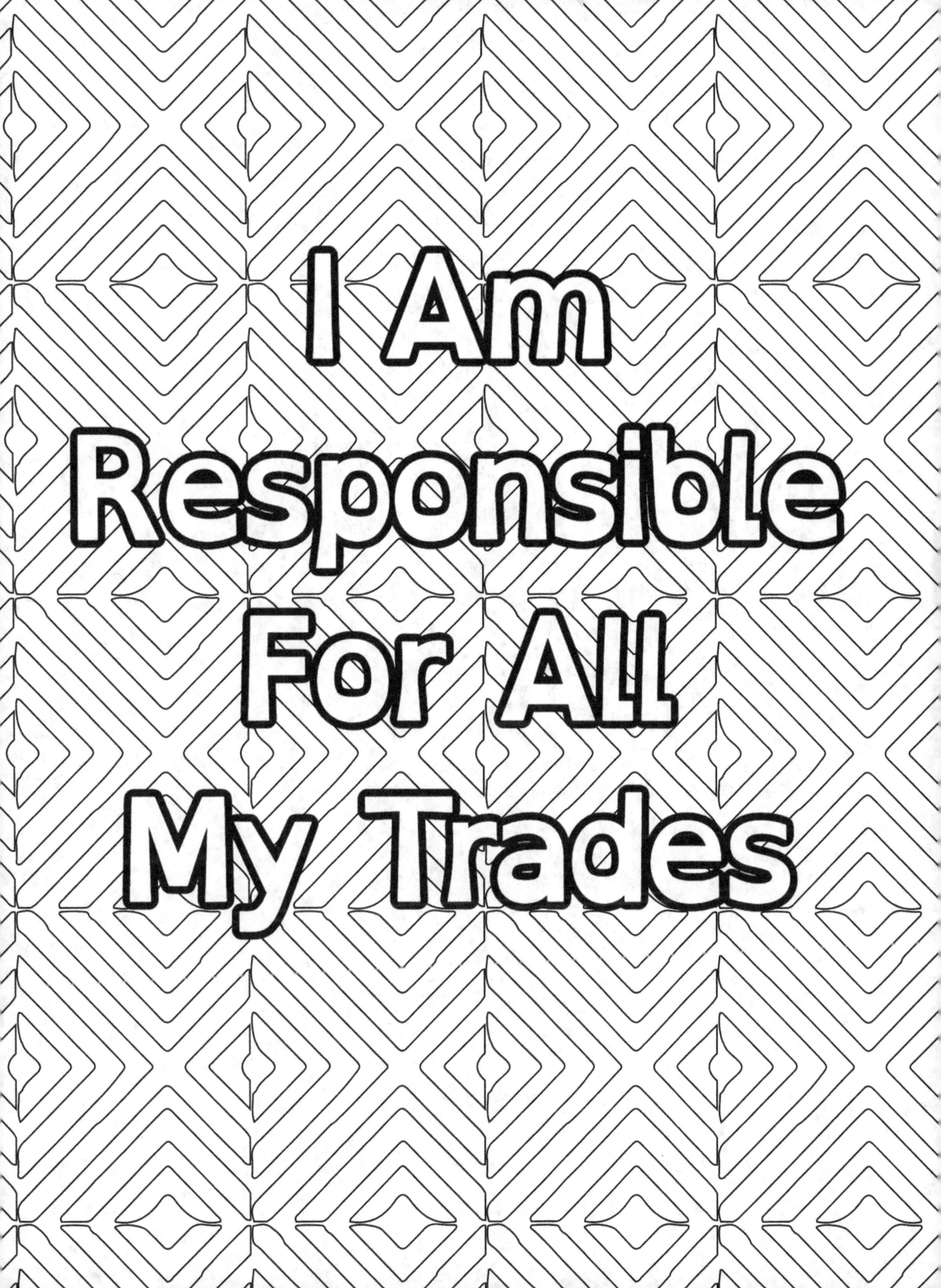

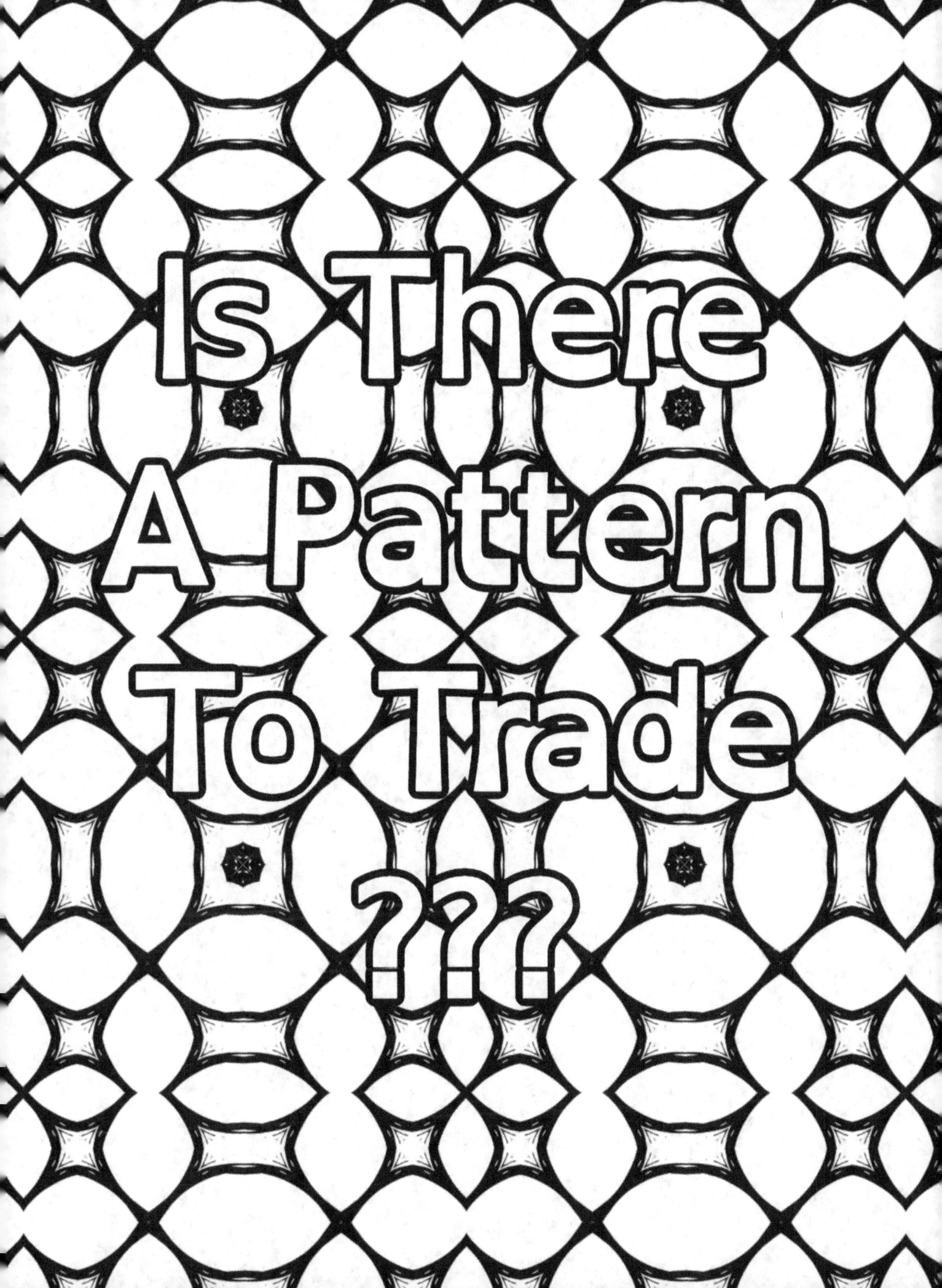

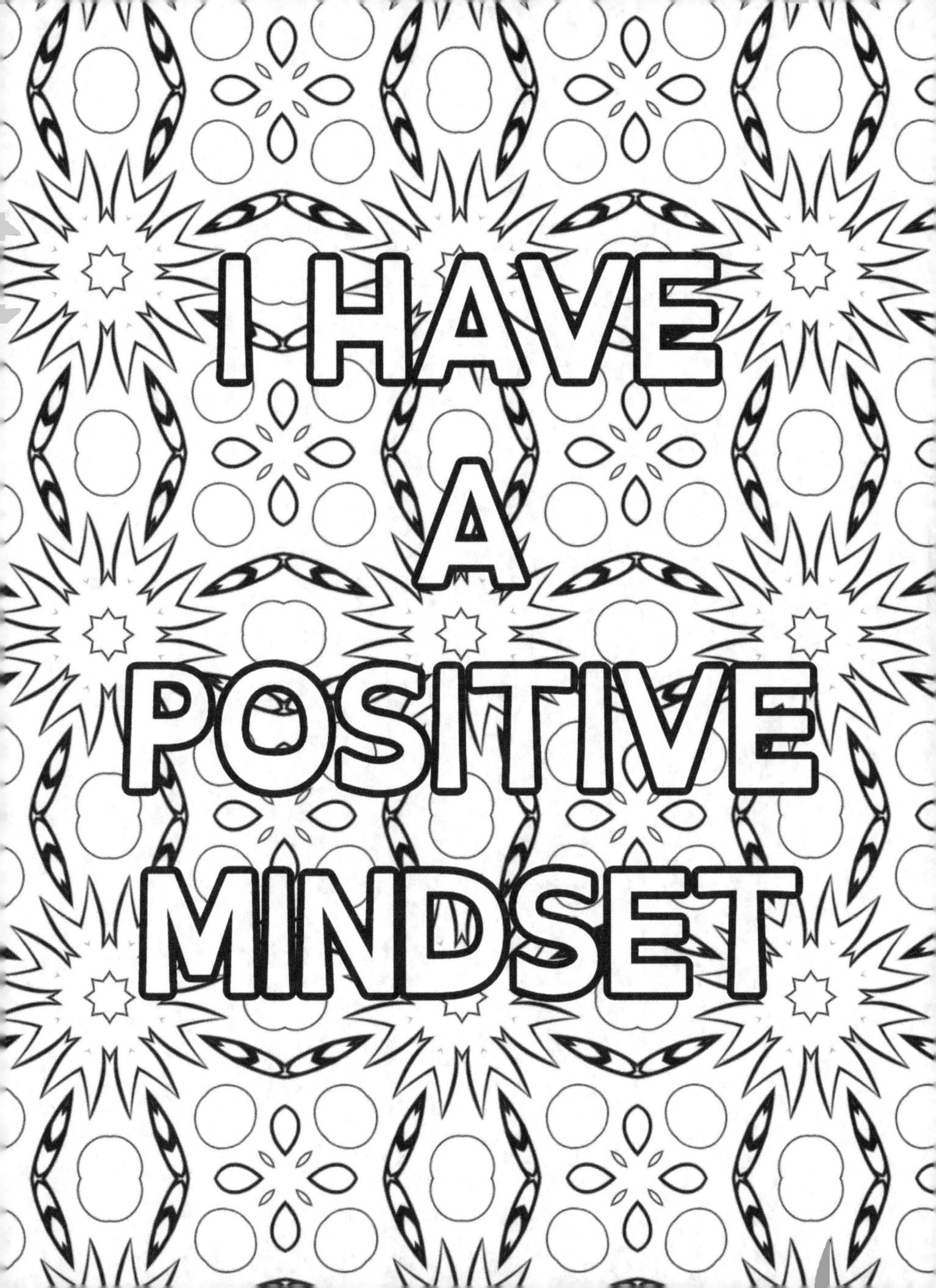

I TAKE BREAKS FROM TRADING

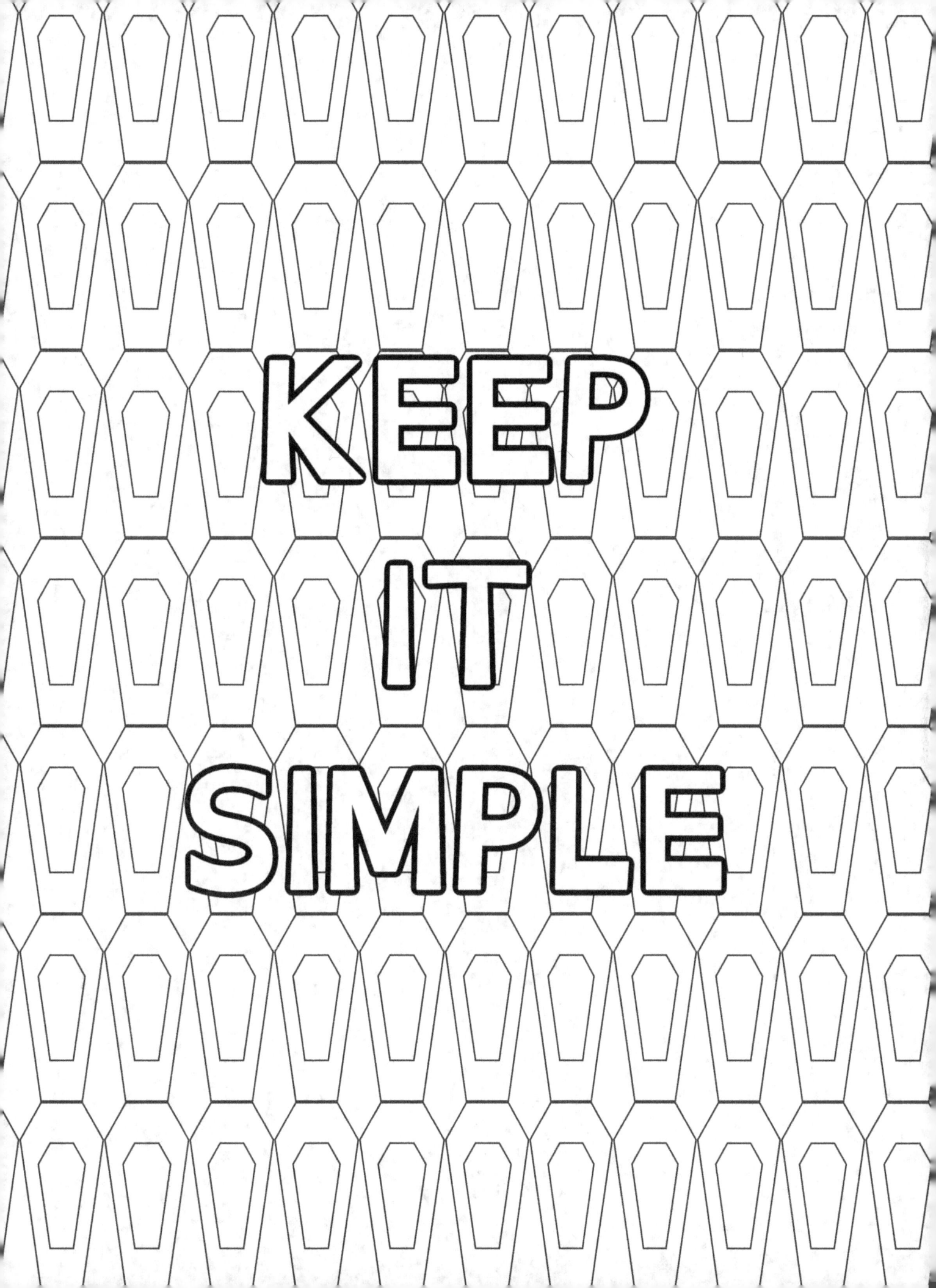

I Remove Emotion From Trading

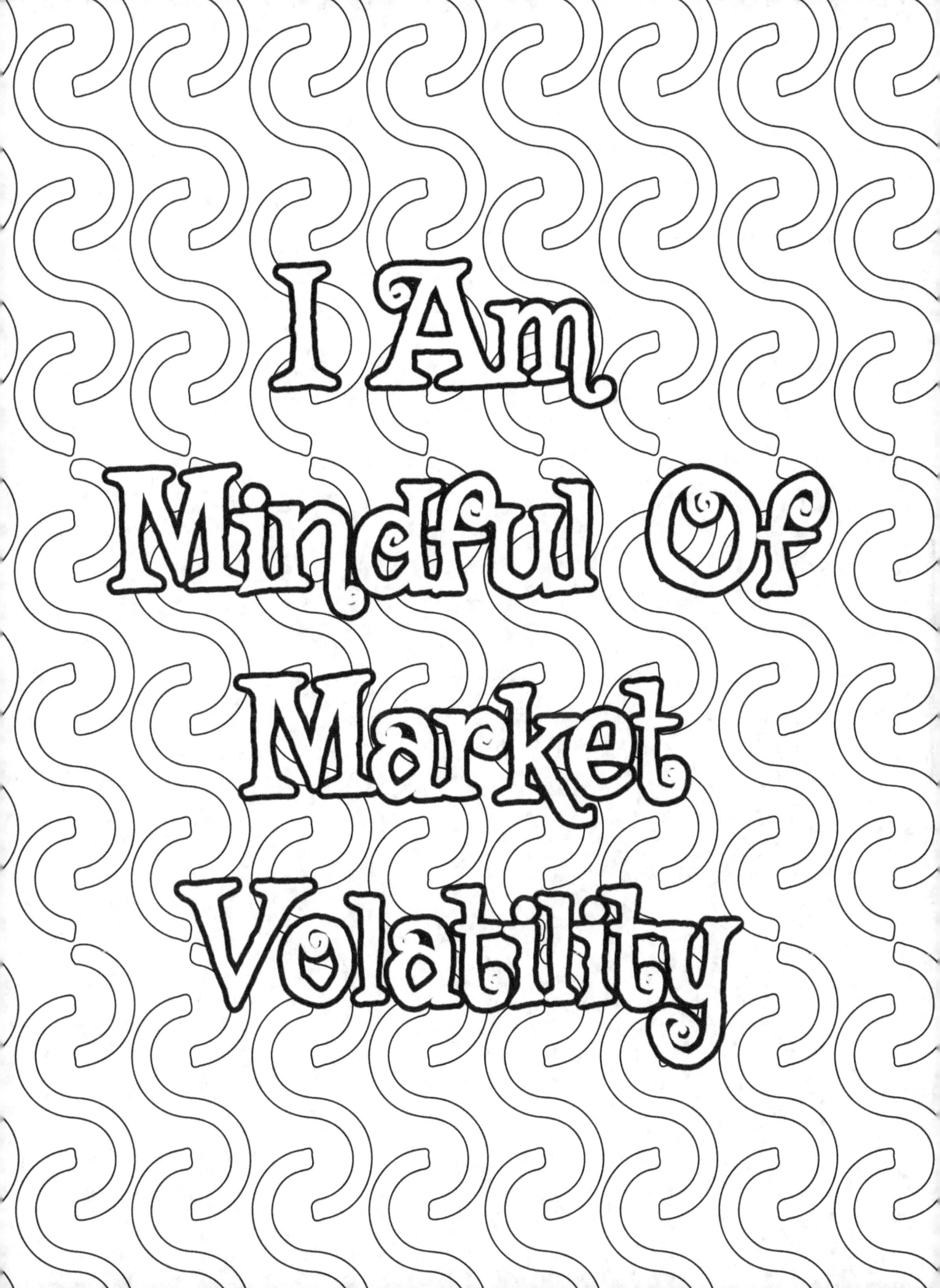

Don't Put Everything In One Basket